LITTLE JOHNNY PLAYS

HOOPS

EVERYTHING ABOUT BASKETBALL

SPORTS FOR KIDS

Children's Sports & Outdoors Books

BABY PROFESSOR
EDUCATION KIDS

Speedy Publishing LLC
40 E. Main St. #1156
Newark, DE 19711
www.speedypublishing.com

Basketball has become one of the more popular sports of the world. It is played using a hoop and a ball. Points are scored by shooting the ball and getting it through the hoop.

Read further to learn more about the game, its history, its rules and how it is played.

Two basketball players in action.

WHY IS IT SO POPULAR?

There are several reasons that basketball has become such a popular sport to enjoy:

- **It's Fun To Play:** Basketball is a very fast and exciting game, and each player on the court is able to play both defense and offense with the roles of each playing being defined loosely. It is easy to learn since it can be practiced by one person (think dribbling and shooting). It can also be played one-on-one up to 5-on-5, so you do not need a lot of people to get a game started.

- **Equipment Is Simple:** All you need to play is a hoop and a ball. There are many playgrounds that supply the hoops which makes it easy to get a game started as long as you have a ball.

- **It's Fun To Watch:** The game has lots of excitement, is fast-paced, and there is usually a lot of scoring. Many great athletes are basketball players. Who is your favorite?

- **It's An All-Weather Sport:** While often played outside in driveways or parks, it can also be played indoors during winter, so it can be enjoyed all year round.

Young basketball players playing with energy.

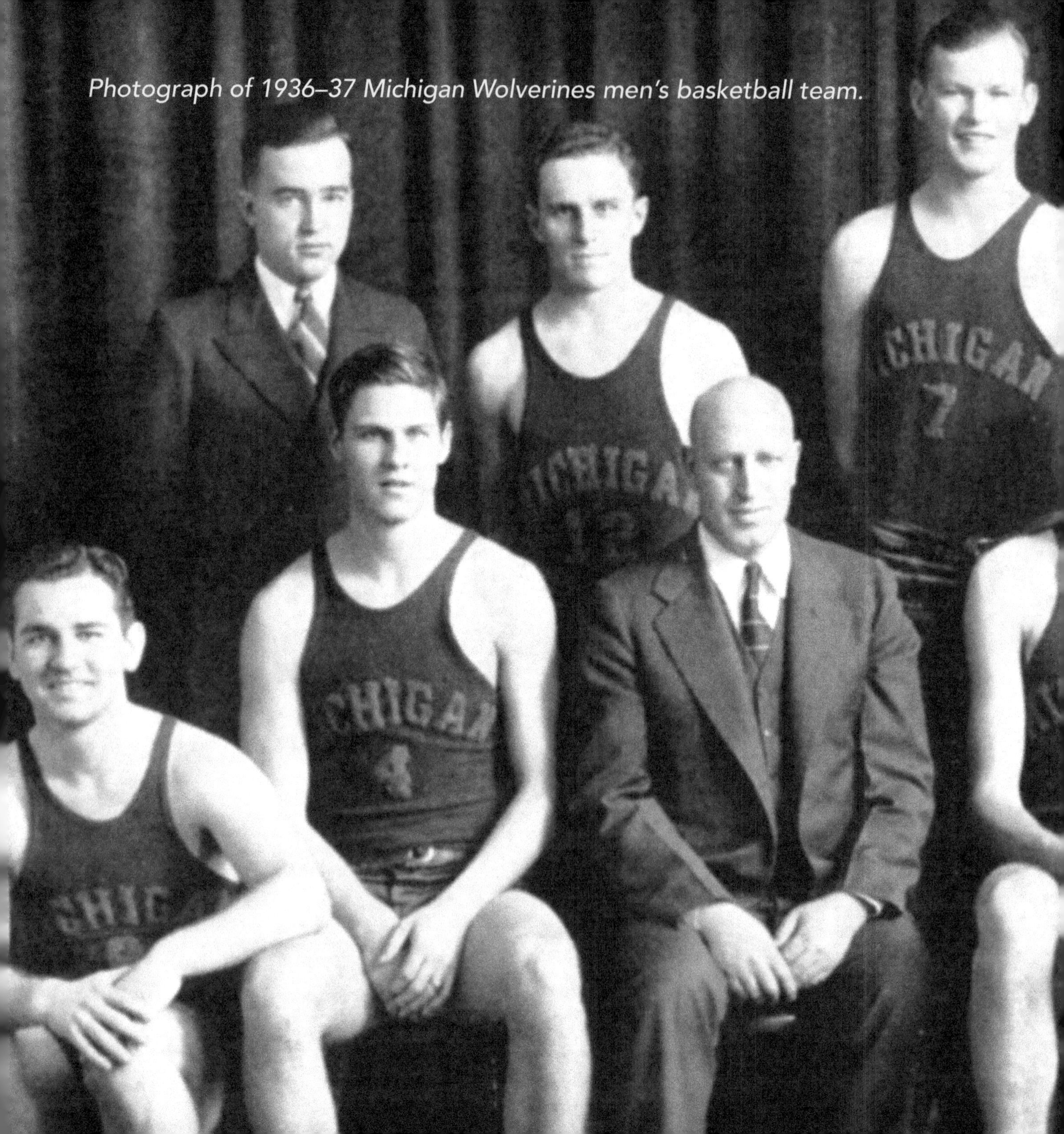
Photograph of 1936–37 Michigan Wolverines men's basketball team.

HISTORY

Jim Naismith invented basketball in 1891 for an indoor sport to be played during the cold Massachusetts winter at the local YMCA. Originally, it was played with two peach baskets and a soccer ball.

It soon began to spread from the local YMCA to colleges where the first leagues were formed. Once it gained in popularity at the college level, the professional leagues began to form. Basketball then became an Olympic sport in 1936. The National Basketball Association (NBA) is one of the more popular professional leagues in today's sports world.

Gatorade
Budweiser
JORDAN 97
WILKINS 145
PLR F PTS
PLR F PTS
Gatorade
THIRST QUENCHER
Winston
Enjoy Coca-Cola
BULLS 23
Gatorade Slam-Dunk Championship

Basketball has had many players that helped to make it popular as a spectator sport, including, but not limited to, Oscar Robinson, Wilt Chamberlain, Larry Bird, and Magic Johnson. Probably the most famous and the greatest player of all time has to be Michael Jordan.

Game Time Basketball.

RULES

The rules vary slightly dependent upon the play level, or where the game is being played. However, these differences are typically only variations of the basic game and most of the rules referenced below can apply to just about any game of basketball.

The team that gets the most points is the winner. Points are scored by tossing the basketball through the opponent's basket or hoop. During regular play, when a basket is scored within the three-point line, it is worth 2 points and a basket scored from outside the three-point line gets 3 points. If a player gets a free throw in the basket, it is 1 point.

Basketball game strategy on blackboard.

RULES FOR THE OFFENSE

The team that has possession of the basketball is the offense. There are certain rules that apply to a player that has control over the basketball:

1. He must dribble (bounce) the basketball using one hand as both feet are moving. At any time, if both hands touch it or he stops dribbling it, he can only move one foot. The stationary foot is referred to as the pivot foot.

2. He can only dribble the ball for one turn, meaning that if he has stopped dribbling, he cannot start to dribble again. If he starts dribbling again, he is called for a double-dribble violation and loses the ball to the opposing team. A player is only able to start dribbling again after another player from his team or the opposing team touches or gains control of it. This typically occurs after a pass or a shot.

3. The ball has to stay in bounds. If a player on the offensive team loses the basketball out of bounds, the other team gains control of it.

SAINT LOUIS
24
TEMPLE
33

4. His hand is required to stay on top of the ball as he is dribbling it. If his hand touches the bottom of it as he is dribbling, and he continues to dribble, this is known as carrying it and the ball is turned over to the opposing team.

5. When the offensive team has crossed half court, they cannot return to the backcourt. This is known as a backcourt violation. If a defensive player knocks the basketball into backcourt, the offensive team can legally recover it.

Basketball player trying to make a pass.

Women's basketball team.

RULES FOR THE DEFENSE

The team that does not have the basketball is the defense.

The chief rule for a defensive player is to not foul. Using physical contact to gain an unfair advantage is known as a foul. While this can be a judgment call on the part of the referee, typically a defensive player is not allowed to touch an offensive player in any way that causes the offensive player to miss the shot or lose it.

Two athletes playing basketball outdoors.

RULES FOR ALL PLAYERS

1. While the foul rule mentioned above was described as a defensive rule, it also applies to all players on the court exactly the same, including the offensive players.

2. A player is not allowed to hit the basketball with their fist or kick the ball.

3. No player is allowed to touch the ball as it is traveling towards the basket or on the rim. This is referred to as goaltending. However, in some games, touching the basketball as it is on the rim can be legal.

Two opposing basketball players.

Every player on the court is subject to the same rules irrespective of their position. There are no positions in the rules, therefore the positions are only for team strategy.

The ball on the basketball court next to the referee.

STRATEGY

As you watch a game on television, sometimes it might seem like there are only a group of players dribbling the basketball around and shooting for the basket. It can appear chaotic at times, but it is very strategic. In fact, teams are playing sophisticated defenses as well as setting up and playing many offensive plays. On the sideline, the coaches are constantly watching the game, ensuring that the right players are in the game, they make adjustments as necessary, and try to outwit the opposing team.

DEFENSIVE STRATEGY

Even though scoring is fun to watch, fun to do, and exciting, the key to winning a basketball game is the defense. The teams will often change the defenses and change the player who might be guarding. Zone defense and man-to-man defense are the two main forms of defenses.

Two healthy basketball players at the playground outdoors.

When each player has a certain area of the court they are responsible for defending, this is known as a zone defense. The zone moves and shifts dependent upon where the offensive players are and the location of the basketball. The zone defense is good for stopping an inside score since several players can surround a player and get the ball from the inside. This defense is not so good for stopping the long shots or outside shots.

When each player has a specific offensive player to cover, this is known as a man-to-man defense. The player guards his assigned offensive player throughout the court. This type of defense can be very effective against a team that has a strong outside shooting team.

Man-to-man also can help with rebounding since each defender blocks out the player they are assigned and no one is able to slip into open zones.

OFFENSIVE STRATEGY

Offensive strategies include plays designed for a certain type of play. The teams may decide to compete in an up-tempo game or they may want to slow it down. The teams with fast and athletic players might intend to play a game that is fast-paced so they are able to take advantage of their speed in open court.

Two athletes playing basketball outdoors.

Passing is the key to a good offensive strategy. The basketball is able to be passed quicker and more effective than if it is dribbled. Passing it around quickly by the offensive team can cause the opposing team to move and make any necessary adjustments. With enough good passes, an offensive player will eventually be able to find a good open shot.

The pick-and-roll is one of the mainstays for almost any offensive game. This occurs when one of the offensive players obstructs a player that is defending a second offensive player that has control of the ball. The player that has control of the ball then starts to move.

At this same time, the player that is setting the pick rolls towards the basket. Now, the defenders have to decide who to cover. Often, they get distracted and either the player with control of the basketball has an open shot, or the player that is setting up the pick will be open for a quick and easy layup.

Basketball going through the hoop at a sports arena.

Basketball is a great sport and a lot of fun for you to play with your friends. Hopefully now that you have learned the rules you can get a game together!

If you need more information about learning to play basketball you can go to your local library, research the internet or ask your gym teacher, family and friends.

Visit

BABY PROFESSOR
EDUCATION KIDS

www.BabyProfessorBooks.com

to download Free Baby Professor eBooks
and view our catalog of new and exciting
Children's Books